chicken + lowercase = fleur

Poems by

Christine Tierney

LILY POETRY REVIEW BOOKS

Copyright © 2021 by Chrstine Tierney

Published by Lily Poetry Review Books
223 Winter Street
Whitman, MA 02382

https://lilypoetryreview.blog/

ISBN: 978-1-7347869-1-0

All rights reserved. Published in the United States by Lily Poetry Review Books.
Library of Congress Control Number: 2020935497

Cover Collage and Design: Martha McCollough

Acknowledgements

great weather for MEDIA: "the birth of lowercase and a ditty for shmummy"

Star 82 Review: "minnowfish"

Permafrost: "sunflower's remains"

Weave Magazine: "scene"

PMS: "the darker" and "getting to white"

Poet Lore: "16 things you should know about the fort"

tNYPress: "why 8" and "rather die than kiss him"

LUNGFULL!: "letter to sunflower in ink-blood and chlorophyll"

The Tusculum Review: "f-f-fit"

The Yalobusha Review: "canarycousin" and "sunflower's binge"

Sleet Magazine: "s-s-sibs"

Skidrow Penthouse: "sunflowers holding out"

Lingerpost: "numbering the gruesome"

The Boiler Journal: "the orange"

The Broome Review: "qu-qu-quench"

Gemini Magazine: "fumes"

Thrice Fiction: "the day lowercase heard her brother tell ricky c he wanted her dead"

shufPoetry: "b-b-bladespeak"

Threadcount: "8th floor" and "lowercase in sunflower headdress"

Fourteen Hills: "thanksgiving murk"

Pismire: "truths and half-truths about sunflowers"

Thank you to my crazy-talented writing group: Frannie Lindsay, Ann Killough, E.B. Moore and Susan Nisenbaum-Becker.

Thank you to the community of friends and mentors whose love and support has helped in ways I never thought possible: Ann Niederkorn, J. Garston, Clifton Adamson, Julia Kanno, Helena Wilson, Aimee Sands, Jim Henle, Kim Garcia, Alan Albert, Tam Neville, Bert Stern, Carla Schwartz, Joe Killough, Taryn Bowe, David Menzies, Everyone from The Brookline Reading Series, Brian Burgess, Emma Mai, Tanya English, Casey Long, Anthony Laiosa, Christen DiBiase, all of my CAPI kids, parents and teachers both past and present, Harold Bond, Elaine Sheer, Jane Katims, Emily O'Neil. Patricia Smith, Jeanne Marie Beaumont, Ted Deppe, Kazim Ali, Annie Finch, Lisa Horowitz and Laura Kotcamp.

Thank you to my father, mother, Dave, Pep, Emily and Austin.

Thank you to Eileen Cleary, the best editor on the flippin' planet, and to Collage and Design artist Martha McCollough for her brilliant work on the cover.

Thank you to Eli Roberts for saving my life by donating one of his kidneys to a total stranger on my behalf as part of the paired kidney exchange.

Thank you to the unknown altruistic donor whose kidney (I named her Rosa Ruby!) is thriving inside of me.

Thank you to Dr. Stephan Tullius, Dr. Shashrit Waikar, Dr. Leonardo Riella, Dr. Karen Siller, Nancy Minghella, Michelle Scala, Annmarie Dunn-Morgan, all of my phlebotomists, and every other kind soul at the Brigham and Women's Hospital who cared for me before, during and after my kidney transplant.

If you are interested in becoming a kidney donor or would like some information about living kidney donation, please contact the kidney donor team at your local hospital or The National Kidney Foundation.

And finally, thank you to the most important person in my life, my one and only true love, Luis Julio Blanco.

Contents

k-k-kin

1. the birth of lowercase and a ditty for shmummy
2. get a friggin' grip
3. minnowfish
4. sunflower's remains
5. scene
6. box
7. the darker
8. k-k-kin
9. wake up, it's easter
10. the ballad of pinkypinky chicken

f-f-fit

13. why 8?
14. how to be a smoothly running robot
15. plump
16. letter to sunflower in ink-blood and chlorophyll
17. f-f-fit
18. 100 day hush
19. listen look stop-stop-stop
20. canarycousin
21. garden/beach/beautiful salmon flame
22. rather die than kiss him
23. two tittle mixed-up poems

s-s-sibs

27. another pitiful tribute to chicken
28. tangle
29. s-s-sibs
30. sunflowers holding out

31	16 things you should know about the fort
32	the bitter house
33	even during the silent treatments, they make noise
34	bacitracin hill
35	not that game
36	11 chapters of lowercase, abridged

qu-qu-quench

39	sunflower's binge
40	the orange
41	just another day in '82
42	qu-qu-quench
44	fumes
45	(hey sunflower, l.c. thinks you might be dead)
46	the day lowercase heard her brother tell ricky c he wanted her dead
47	from haiku to thwack
48	numbering the gruesome
49	like a canker it came running

b-b-bladespeak

53	petal
54	a night by the sink
55	exhuming the thrum
56	thanksgiving murk
57	8th floor
58	lowercase in sunflower headdress
59	off the mark
60	b-b-bladespeak
61	getting to white
62	truths and half-truths about sunflowers

For Luis, who once said to me, "Today, when I was putting something away in your closet, I could smell you everywhere, so I grabbed a bunch of your clothes and buried my face in the smell of you."

k-k-kin

the birth of lowercase and a ditty for shmummy

in seventeen or eighteen minutes a single ray of light ransacked the balding lawn around back and shmummy was kicking lowercase out.

lowercase tried like heck not to tear through shmummy's muddy surface as she pushed, laced her toes through a slat between her ribs, curled her double-jointed pinkie around her kidney.

as shmummy stopped for an irked breath while a hefty aunt who smelled like chicken cutlets massaged her feet, lowercase plopped an eyeball against that stench and scrutinized her future:

pea-green table legs, empty carton of temptee cream cheese, crocheted doll-head toilet cover cozy, and a paint by number of the last supper hanging above the hifi in the dining room.

eviction pressed on. shmummy pushed with the force of an orca, blew a bloody vessel in her right eye and grunted through the sateen bedspread stuffed into her mouth like a gag.

but when lowercase slipped on shmummy's torment and squelched through a molassesy sadness that saw no end——shmummy was pissed. she inhaled lint and cat fur from the sea of shag carpet, and exhaled the la-z-boy with the broken lever.

the force was too much. lowercase never wanted out. she grabbed and grabbed and held nothing. she clawed without claws, without bones, without muscles, and held nothing.

lowercase busted a tiny gut trying not to upset ol' shmummy, and soon enough this tug and pull became their song.

get a friggin' grip

this ain't no rose, no sickly-sweet lilac
just a slump that imposes with its bend
and hogs all the sun. still, l.c.'s compelled
to figure this one out, she's a sucker

for hidden beauty; the dank-fatty pores,
the s.o.s.y limbs and the parts that poke
like the curled in tips of burnt stars.
every day since this obsession began

l.c. has been pacing the grounds
where they spawn; digging
into everything like a crack rabbit.

big, brooding, scentless fleurs
the death of them everywhere
and her sumptuous love
for their jaw-dropping corpses.

minnowfish

lowercase sits at the kitchen table drawing her signature puppies, heavy, black-circled cheeks, great lap of a tongue. lowercase's mother dries the last dish, covers what's left of the pot roast with a sheet of aluminum foil and joins her at the table. lowercase's mother crayons a red fish and begins cutting it out with lowercase's pint-sized scissors. *remember the minnowfish at pepper lake*, says lowercase's mother, *how they shimmered?* lowercase slouches. lowercase's mother continues cutting. the refrigerator whirs; the strawberry clock above the stove burbles. again, lowercase's mother asks her about the fish at pepper lake, and lowercase does not answer. lowercase stares at her mother's beige fingers; distant, tarnished rings. a thick, greasy film settles. lowercase's mother finishes cutting out her fish. the hovering light is excruciatingly yellow. lowercase's mother gets up from the kitchen table and places the fish in lowercase's lap and says, *i'm done*. lowercase sits with the flimsy minnow congealed in quiet. lowercase's mother unties her faded apron and dissolves from the kitchen like organdy mist. lowercase holds the paper creature up to the dangling light. the minnowfish curls in the pulse of her hand, and flops to the floor, a bloodless appendage.

sunflower's remains

the season of lava and anguish
is gone, and she is nothing
but feathery husk.

l.c. sweeps the porch.
a light spray of frost
crosses rotting boards,
and there she is,
everything on mum's face
eaten, half-eaten. she has
finally become the uncolor

l.c. desires; if only gray or soot
could fully describe this.
if only l.c. could have been there
as each incisor pierced, sunk,
her fairness giving in, her sepals
bucking, the horror of the clouded light.

l.c. stops sweeping to hold her.
mum's crisp head warbles
on a tress of shriveled wheat.
l.c.'s fingers whiten, thunder into numb,

and with this raw unfelt
she will edge into every fissure
of autumn until the weeping begins.

scene

the woman in the kitchen plays mother.
she rinses blood from a limp chicken,
and shakes a box of green flakes over raw potatoes.

out in the living room lowercase gums
the worn edge of a wooden block.

if only the woman could step out of the kitchen,
forget about the tuck and rub
of the dead bird, manipulate a new prop,

feign something unscripted with her hands.

box

*

corrugated paper siding

it was never known
what sent mum
into the box, some say
the empty ice-trays,
others, the bone-dry meatloaf.

*

as tall as the dresser

stayed there for days.
pumice stone circling
the roughs of her elbows,
lotion leaching into
the crannies of her feet.

*

FRAGILE stamped in red

patient little lowercase,
plunked on the floor in the den,
lining up her porcelain teacups
along the woolen braid of the rug.

*

four flaps opening and closing

but then again,
there were moments
of swaying sunflowers,
tangy pink-lemonade
set with matching pink straws.

the darker

she could tell you a thing or two about feeling like there are no feelings—about summertime and dandelions—about weeds that she called poppies, weeds that she called space suds that sprung up all over a father's patchy lawn—she could confess that she called calla lilies tiger lilies and vice versa, and how the green whips jutting from their middles reminded her of sour apple bubblegum—she could tell you a thing or two about wearing ribbed polyester shorts when everyone else had moved on to denim—about the difference between pig and ponytails: how one was pulled tight to expose your fat face and the other hung loose on your shoulders so you could breathe and chew taffy without headaches—she could write a book about a brother who could make so much noise about how much she weighed, tell you how every fight ended with her fat, and how back then that was all it took to end everything—if she wanted to she could tell you how it felt to sit in the dark of some broken-down closet and think of every single comeback—she could tell you—no she could whisper—how in the absence of light fat becomes nothing more than heat

k-k-kin

eerily, the rush of polyethylene
and guilt skulks down the splintered
seam of the plastic rug runner.
headaches galore. noses flamed
in azure-wisp and ruby. baby
powder caked beneath flabby pits.
it wasn't supposed to be like this:
breaths held like dead mice,
tails decomposing in tuckered
hands, *get out of your goddam room
and empty the vase.* the sunflowers
are unresponsive. septic. sludged.
so sludged. they're unable to mask the stench
of family from their unwashed hair.

wake up, it's easter

this is lowercase, and this is mum.
keep it down cuz mum's still sleeping.

this is mum's dainty snore,
and this is the joyless blue of mum's eyes
dripping onto the matted fur of her terry robe.

this is the shoebox where they now
have to live. it's dark inside the shoebox
and lowercase is salivating for eggy things.

mum forgot the ham.
repeat. mum forgot the ham.

this is lowercase dreaming
about rings of canned pineapple
stuck to someone else's pig.

this is dad ripping the phone out of the wall
and smashing all of the corelle dinner plates
the day mum and lowercase moved into the shoebox.

mum also forgot; the hollow chocolate bunny,
the jelly beans, the windup baby chick, the peeps,
and the netted bag of jacks.

the ballad of pinkypinky chicken

***

her belly holds me. i'm a nosynosy guppy. i spy as mummymummy knits square after square of soon-to-be soon-to-be afghans.

***

daddy's pinto chortles up the street, a million tools rattlerattle in the back. i kickykicky hard. i kickykicky rockemsockem robot hard, and mummymummy drops her clacky needles in between the cushions of the couch.

***

mummymummy pats down the poof in her uncombeduncombed hair, and steals the last smidgensmidgen of red rose tea from her priceypricey gold-rimmed teacup when she hears daddy's-breaks-halt!

***

janglejangle go daddy's keys as he godzilla stomps up the creakycreaky front steps. before daddy's mitt turns the handle of the warpywarpy screen door, mummymummy drags me in her swollenswollen belly to the kitchen where we quickyquicky check on dinner.

***

mummymummy stabs the tarnished fork tines into the chicken's plumpyplumpy, way too plumpy, why so plumpy breast, and panics as the pinkypinky juices ooze on out.

***

i stop squirming--ungently nudging, and mummymummy cranks the heat up high. cracklecrackle-spitspit-smokesmoke. more smoke. daddy's in the archway breathing firefire.

f-f-fit

why 8?

so, if mean pervy gerald dropped a garter snake down the back of your tucked in t-shirt you'd what, call the pigs? maybe you'd scream like big ol' pussy or flap your arms around like a wuss-bag. not l.c., she's that rusted frickin' lock on mr. migalachi's door which no one in the neighborhood can pick. she's that gargantuan rock with the spray-painted smiley face dicks that the marlboro light puffing posers make-out on. see, even when the majorettes were chanting in l.c.'s head, *hey hey fatties don't tuck-in. no, no, fatties don't tuck-in,* she didn't move one flabby muscle. she counted in 8's instead. 8 stabs of light from between the branches of the turdtar trees. 8 snaky thrashes against her velveteen love handles, and she thinks she even counted 8 little snickers from her douchey cousin kate with the titmouse feet who rubbed her smelly spit against her double-jointed thumb declaring, *soul sisters forever.* but what stands out most about that day mean pervy gerald dropped that god-damned garter snake down the back of l.c.'s tucked in t-shirt is how for at least 8 friggin' minutes after she hit the deck, she tasted something like blood and cheese curls eddying around in her shit-shy mouth.

how to be a smoothly running robot

1. wink at clock (who looks like a teapot) and begin.
2. tighten the screws around your wrists. check and double-check the hardware on your elbows and finger-hinges.
3. clang the big spoon, sharpen the good knife and place the metallic pots with the shiny copper bottoms on top of the stove.
4. unwrap, rinse, pound, chop, mince, season, and fuss with knobs.
5. when the buzzer sounds and the smell of pork roast shellacs the house, whip the potatoes with your electric mixer hand, and toss hunks of margarine into the nibblet corn.
6. when the fleshy-things assemble, try not to look at them even though you are programmed to do so.
7. after serving, take your place at the table.
8. bite down on your tinny tongue as the big-gutted fleshy-thing says grace, and the little fleshies bow their heads, but never join them in prayer.
9. listen carefully as the clock codes its love for you in ticks.
10. sit before your untouched plate until the fleshy-things finish.
11. blow a little kiss to clock as the fleshy things fight like jackals over the last buttermilk biscuit.

plump

first, she was thrust from purple hole

then she was fed until she was plump

still plump, she went to school and smiled wide, even when she didn't want to, so the kids would stop calling her sasquatch

it didn't work

someone wrote, *beware of sasquatch* on her desk, and someone else wrote, *ha*, below it

at the mdc pool, she wore a long, baggy t-shirt over her bathing suit in the water and told everyone it was because she was allergic to chlorine

no one freaking believed her

she made a tiny friend with a tiny name called amy, and put up with all of her *oh my gosh, my feet are so petite next to yours* digs because she never picked her last for kickball

she got plumper

she tried to unplump by chomping down an apple after every bag of fritos, and running up and down the little bump-of-a-hill in her backyard till she couldn't breathe

but that didn't work either

she thought an awful lot about crawling back inside the purple hole, but she wasn't stupid, she knew she was way too plump to fit back in

letter to sunflower in ink-blood and chlorophyll

lowercase is no one's daughter.
like you, she is stem and rind

slash and leak. in the ground
there was hope, all the water

she could drink. she chewed diamonds
down there! things get old quick.

corollas fold in, the rest
falls out. lowercase was someone's

luminary once, wasn't she?
do you know why the razzly-

most dazzly skies are so tenebrous?
didn't think so.

oh, lonesome butterpelt, oh, pandora
of gaping gapes, lowercase could be yours.

she could be gussied up and sung to.
she could be your babylily, your easter-

basket, your teensy pair of eyelet gloves.

f-f-fit

l.c. just started gasping, panting like a tuckered-out pooch rasping. they were out driving on a country road. pine trees, braided sky, chipped barns, fruit stands. *pull over*, she yelled, *shmummy, pull over.* lowercase staggered off into the woods like a broken gazelle, searched high and low for air, and hid behind a sprawling bush. if tears are water parks! if blood is thick! her face, a soaked t-shirt heaped beside the tub. lowercase gulped and choked like a codfish flopping on a splintered deck. she stopped to rest and tried like heck to catch her breath then spotted a little yellow flower at her feet. she crouched to look at it close up, and it spit at her. a brown sticky molassesy spit eeled across her cheek. she broke a monster sweat trying to yank the little yellow flower from the ground, but couldn't. the flower bit the tip of her thumb with teeth that looked like claws. blueblack blood trickled down, so she planted a big sugary peck on the flower's ghastly maw. then it was the flower's turn. it hawked and hacked and coughed up its little flower lung. lowercase thought she might be looking into a magic mirror. she sat patiently gazing at the flower's buttery petals curling in out and her naughty breath returned. worried that shmummy was worried, she sprung up, brushed the blobs of dirt and grass from the bum of her shorts, and skedaddled back to the car where shmummy was busy working on her crosswords.

100 day hush

curled-up feast of paint chips
on the dirty, dirty sill.
pubey permed hair clumped in the drain.
steel blue swivel rocker
rooted to her her spot.
it's either extra chunky jiff or nothing.
lucky chinese elephants
and wanna-be-hummels-
all acting up!
shades down. lights off.
thunder of amber whisky
crashing against sputtering rocks.
growing ball of snotty tissues.
sqealing lazy-susan.
wild cherry sucret wrappers
jammed into pepsi cans.
4 white stones left on the porch.
damp, molding laundry left by the dryer.
bits of nailclippings on untouched toast.
velvet lined jewelry box
crammed with smelly milk teeth.

listen look stop-stop-stop

watch. l.c. shuffle. half-jump. shuffle. she's down. damaged. rice paper knee twirling violet. violent. don't touch l.c.'s shoulders; she hates it when you touch her shoulders. don't ask her how this world blew to smithereens. she's no doll. no dimple. no faulty porcelain blink. see l.c. she's limping around the swing set. round and round she goes. shiver of branches. startle of skywash. chafed. no chase. she's hiding behind the towering snowbank. don't count. her fingers turn chagallybruseyblue. she never asks to play. l.c. doesn't ask. fur-lined gloves. icestiff. ravenous grackles. starveling trees.

canarycousin

lowercase is beginning to write dinky, gerbil hair dinky.
every letter no bigger than a sip.
oh, little dylan, get out your magnifying glass,
and amplify me. make me as grand as a jesus-halo.
make me larger than my crappo life." lowercase has always been big,
though she's much smaller than she used to be.
last night, a lady told her when she sees her old shorts
they look like a slice of toast, *because that's how small i was back then.*
lowercase doesn't have any of her old shorts,
but they were bigger than the whole loaf.
they were brown and mud-green and husky, not like her cousins
that were lemony and chirpy and itty-bitty like a canary.
one boring day, when lowercase and her friends
were all out back by the birdbath, (no birds in sight),
someone in shorts much smaller than hers
dared her to knock over the birdbath which was full of wet leaves
and twigs, and even sludgy worms, so she did,
and it smashed and cracked all over the place.
what she didn't know, was that her father had been spying on her
from the kitchen window, probably shocked
she had actually gone through with it. he tapped-tapped-tapped
on the window pane and all of the bony kids ran
including lowercase's itty-bitty canarycousin
in her polliwog-so-teeny-they-could-fit-in-the-slit-of-your-hip-pocket shorts.
lowercase, well she just stood there by the remaining
stump-of-a-birdbath, and took what she always took
for her scraggy friends. now she practices writing
really really small so she can cram all of her fat thoughts
onto one stinking page.

garden/beach/beautiful salmon flame

the woman next door with the tawny curls
said, *get rid of it, it's strangle weed.*
and do it quick! or all of those sunflowers will die.
so, for two days' l.c. studied
its workaday green
and cunning sway.
she even spotted one slithering
to the top of the neighbors
pine tree. but when has l.c. ever
trusted women? the baby,
the friggin' bath water,
the urge to drown and then cover it up
with a bit of rouge.
once upon a devil's ringlet
l.c.'s big sister dragged
her spumy white carcass
along the lonely shore
of broken crab husks
and beer bottle sea glass.
she doused l.c. in baby oil,
propped her up on a pile of faded blue jeans
and left her to roast
while she sucked face with the boy from 118
who wouldn't even spring
for a ten-cent fucking popsicle.
l.c. never amounted to much
on that beach, pink on top of pink
until that one time when she burst
into a beautiful salmon flame,
was rushed to a hospital
where someone with hairy arms
and mickey mouse gloves
stuck a mile-long needle
into her dimpled butt cheek
to keep her from turning to ash.

rather die than kiss him

big ronnie drew a line across the road with a piece of wet crumbly chalk and told lowercase and her weakling friends they were no longer allowed to cross it unless one of them kissed him hard on his always-smeared-with-ropey-spit-mouth because big ronnie was an asswipe who lowercase made an effort to like because they were both chunky, although he was much chunkier than her and his skin looked like hamburger pizza. lowercase tried bribing big ronnie and his band of twisted albeit loyal minions into letting them cross the road with her double jointed thumb turkey dances, and the only one wooed by her bizarro offerings was big ronnie's gabbling cousin who clapped and sang "seven" which lowercase thought meant seven more times, but it didn't, and he sang it over and over until big ronnie licked and puckered his slimy-come-and-smooch-me-lips and lowercase pretended to gag, so he snapped his pork rind fingers and his seven-singing dolt cousin whacked her in the tit with a slat of wood with something sharp on the end of it and a blood blister that she waited almost two weeks to show her mother nearly killed her. one night, lowercase and bucktoothed marna revolted by beheading every prized white lilac from big ronnie's mother's lilac bush and shredded them into limp confetti and left the sweet soggy bones right there for big ronnie's fat eyes to see. a few months later, big ronnie's heart exploded into pissy bits of lard smathered in bosco sauce and his mommy dearest mother wiped a tsunami of black goop from her steely eyes at the wake where lowercase was forced to attend and dress up for. big ronnie's sister, crazy carol, had to pinch her thick tattooed arm with her pointed eggplant nails to get herself to cry while big ronnie's brother jib, the only lanky one in the brood, just didn't show. when it was lowercase's turn at the coffin she cried for that orca, not because she felt shitty that he was dead, but because all she could think about when she looked down at his blubbery face and eerie spitless lips that she would have gladly slit her wrists with a butter knife before kissing, was how mean he was to her, a fellow fatty who needed an ally in this sucky world of skinny minnies.

two tittle mixed-up poems

hunt
in case you were asking—this painting is by magritte.
in case you were asking—she was sent here to answer
the question of fish. you ask why she picks through the trash
for paperclip-wallpaper-necklaces? did you hear a mum
was found on a beach? can you hear mum's gills, mum's fins
or mum's withering scales? lonely-flop. lonely-flop.

mason jar with sunflowermumfish
up to its thick rim in flower. oh, glassy one, don't slip
off the fin-slippery table. but sunflowermumfish elbows on in,
thinks she can tango with the real mums. she can. no, she can't.
l.c. feels nuts, like a sunflower's stripy achenes embedded
in the tread of a hulking boot. she hears a half-mom was found
on a beach and that everyone who loved her has drowned.
stem, pixie cut, seedrich mouth. gurgleflop. gurgleflop.

s-s-sibs

another pitiful tribute to chicken

1—lowercase was raised on jaundiced chicken.

2—lowercase's mum was a sick moth in a quilted pink bathrobe that smelled like vick's vapor rub and white shoulders dusting powder.

3—lowercase heard her older brother tell her older sister he wished the stupid chicken could at least be fried once in a while.

4—lowercase's mum might have had all kinds of beautiful inside her, but who the hell knew.

5—all lowercase's dad did was bark at lowercase's mum. *get a friggin' job down at the goddam bus station with me*, the last place on earth a sick moth could hold a friggin' job.

6—drained and weary, lowercase's mum tore off to arkansas in her 67-convertible mustang with the kicked-in taillight while lowercase was out raking leaves with her friend betty.

7—the day lowercase's mum split, lowercase's dad dragged a mound of sallow chicken out into the living room.

8—lowercase's older brother got the biggest piece, and lowercase's older sister got seconds.

9—lowercase fed her measly scrap of rank chicken to the leg-humping dog.

tangle

their glum world was the inside
of count chocula's coffin,
tasseled ghostpink housecoat
and bitten sticks of wrigley's
spearmint gum. bronchial
and inflamed, their tongues coated
in a cable-knit of lonesome.
if only they were taught
how to leave the last smidgen
of frosting in the fractured bowl.
biggirl snatching fleecy snippets
mum tore from the vexed boule,
dad kneeling on that clammy
lawn, praying for the right-
sized wrench to fall from mary kay
smirched sky. dotty's sponge
curlers reeked of living room
shag, and the living room shag reeked
of *hug me and i'll go postal.*
then came the coterie
of bougiemums wielding
their fiercely mayoed salads
and celery eye cream, gawking
like bulls at the heaps of charred
legos and kfc wet-naps,
shrouding the linoleum
like germicidal petticoats.

s-s-sibs

tthis is what big sunflower said to baby sunflower.

no scalpel. no syringe. no swabs of any kind. no alcohol or peroxide. no sutures. no padding of any sort. no overhead light. no saw for the thicker part. no disinfectant for the surface. no band-aids. no gauze. no tweezers. no muzzle.

but in order to do such a thing big sunflower knew that baby sunflower should be dead, or at least half-dead, so he waited a few days for her to wither and die, or almost die, but that didn't happen.

well, said big sunflower, *i am hungry and cannot wait.*

big sunflower got out his rusty buck knife and cut into baby sunflower's palish calf. he cut clean into it, as clean as purell, and sliced her scrawny leg right off. the leg squinched and jittered on the dirt even though it was no longer attached to her wee body.

that was it. big sunflower booked it to the corner store for a chipwich, and baby sunflower picked up her scrawny leg and tottered off behind him.

sunflowers holding out

on thursdays, they come to lowercase and beg,
staggering on their gooey stalks.

water, one cries. *sun,* another.
she knows what they want and refuses.

they feign with their marigold wisps
craning to and from the light.

she waits as their necks sag
and their peach-sop spines reek;

they are not fit for this kind of heat.
just tell me why i want to hurt you, lowercase demands.

a grudge on each face, a sphincter clamped
and not one single petal released.

pathetic, snarls lowercase. they smirk,
complain, and furl their gunky gills

as she drags their sludge-muck vase
to the center of the darkening room.

16 things you should know about the fort

(1) everything planted near the fort either died or disappeared.

(2) l.c.'s brother built the fort with a bunch of gross stuff he found in a dumpster. he hammered scraps of carpet on the walls that smelled like pee and orange soda.

(3) the fort was shabby.

(4) l.c. sorta loved the fort.

(5) l.c.'s brother's friend bobby lived in the fort for a while.

(6) l.c.'s father wanted bobby to go back home, but he buttered her father up by raking leaves and plucking the occasional dandelion from the lawn.

(7) bobby moved from the fort and into the basement where he slept with the silverfish.

(8) fights broke out over the fort. l.c.'s mother said she'd tear it down herself if she had to. l.c.'s father stored his tools in it.

(9) l.c.'s mother grabbed her keys and tore off in a fern-green mustang because of the damn fort. *enough is enough*, she cried.

(10) bobby sat in the fort and chugged budweiser beer he stole from the old fridge in the basement—sometimes l.c. would join him.

(11) l.c. rarely spent time in the fort alone, but when she did, she thought about her mother's jingling bracelets.

(12) one day bobby saw l.c. stab her brother in the thigh with a fork she'd been eating grapefruit wedges with.

(13) on a tuesday, l.c.'s mother phoned, but no one could find her. she was in the fort with her arms crossed.

(14) bobby took l.c. for a boat ride on the lake. when they were almost out to the middle of the lake, he told her she has a beautiful mouth.

(15) the day bobby moved out he drew a mustache on l.c.'s face with a black sharpie.

(16) it took three days for l.c.'s sharpie mustache to fade. the fort was a good place to hide until it disappeared.

the bitter house

daddy is a hungry walrus
he has awesome tusks and blubber galore
daddy wants his goddamn dinner

mummy is a crumpled tissue waiting to be thrown out
she has a runny nose that never stops running
mummy wants to make a nest in the rafters and sleep

lowercase loves everyone in the house, even tippy the mean cat
she has eyepokey bangs that someone needs to cut
lowercase wants mummy to make daddy his goddamn dinner

daddy calls out
daddy calls out louder

a grueling silence follows

lowercase impales her bottom lip with her two strong buckteeth
until she sees christmas

even during the silent treatments, they make noise

hurled knees against shag carpet.
tv dinners, foil tops crushed into hockey pucks.
ponytails with scraggled seams torn up the back.
l.c.'s dad scraping mac and cheese from a cold pot.
for three days, they'd swipe pennies from the decanter in the pantry.
for three days, they'd pretend mum wasn't in her room.
breakfast on the coffee table in the den.
sword fights with hot wheels' tracks and slotted spoons.

bacitracin hill

in cotton briefs and rhinestone
froggy t-shirt, lowercase zooms above a blaze
of green shag and shmancy velvet
couch pillows in her high-water toughskins.
jean nate splashes gi joe,
who can't seem to keep his fists
off of lowercase's gardenia powder puff.
not again! mr. jumpy's crammed
headfirst into the little drawer of lowercase's plastic
vanity table, his wonky paw spilling out
and feeling around for his lily of the valley
ray gun. marathon bar mustache smeared
across the "guests only" hand towel.
bubble yum bomb explodes in lowercase's spit pointy pigtail,
and she cuts it out (snip!) with her sister's zigzaggy
scissors. lowercase picks the fifty-cent padlock
on her brother's bedroom door where bob seger, van halen,
molly hatchett and bowie are peeling
the electric cherry paper from his walls,
and yuck, the b.o. in this dump is making
the sunflowers shimmy off of lowercase's
always-wedgied-tennis shorts. eight minutes later,
shmum's hauling them off to nana's house
for a whole week of goulash and jiffy pop
just because dad was out all-night chasing
wild turkeys and now "presto"
he's the great smasher of raspberry light bulbs
and scooby doo jelly jars. a swish of fuchsia
contact paper makes almost everything
smell better. "boo-boos!" they all cry,
sliding down bacitracin hill in their skivvies.

not that game

fragments of elk stirring
in the soft wood paneling.

he'd pin her down on the scratchy
green shag, grab her cheeks with his blond

hooves, and stretch em' until the bitty cracks
on her lips split wide. *say puddy tat.*

she'd fight it. *say puddy tat.* she'd twist
and squirm, jerk her head from side to side.

say it, pig, and i'll stop. he'd lower a milky line
of drool from his stormy, metallic mouth,

and then suck it back up before it landed.
the smell. the gunky bits stuck

in-between. the weight of a boys' boundless fury
draped across the length of her.

this was not that game. he was not
the boy who stopped. *if you don't say it i'll punch you.*

he was no dumb buck. knew where to hide
his bronco marks. sometimes she'd end up saying it.

mostly not. either way, his hot acrid breath,
brutebone cloots, landed on her anyway.

10 chapters of lowercase, abridged

chapter 1
l.c. stole 11 ruby sequins from mummy's unused taffeta dress, wrapped them in a wad of toilet paper, and hid them inside her dolly's tiny, floral underpants.

chapter 2
for one whole summer l.c. held a wet pebble in her hand and it never dried.

chapter 3
the clinkety-clink of da dipping into the bottles of grog in the basement sent mummy into her cedar-lined hope chest to shiver.

chapter 4
the shag carpeting itchtickled the spaces between l.c.'s double-jointed toes.

chapter 5
butchie-boy edwards downed a half-gallon of clorox bleach on the same day marty dion held a brass plated magnifying glass over a pile of dirt-dry leaves, and almost burned the frigging barn down.

chapter 6
mummy gave da the silent treatment.

chapter 7
da said, *here we go again with the goddamn silent treatment.*

chapter 8
l.c. peeled a blob of purple bubblegum from her hand-painted headboard and rechewed it.

chapter 9
l.c.'s dumb brother dared her to smash the fred flintstone cookie jar onto da's new lino floor.

chapter 10
l.c. laughed (and peed a little too) when da whacked her in the bum with a kentucky fried chicken drumstick for ruining his new lino floor.

qu-qu-quench

sunflower's binge
after dorothea tanning's "the mirror"

she bends into this bulbed reflection
where there are no secrets,
and rough hair gets rougher.
but it's more than her face she attempts.
more than her face that locks her into
this curse of hot-fake-light,
where pores swell wide enough
for gauded fists, and each fatty seed is coaxed
and then bullied out.
it is here that her world is smeared
beyond recognition, and oily fingertips
prod without consent. this tasty gunmetal,
this silverfish of silverfish is the center of all
she's convinced is broken.

the orange

sits on her dashboard
it has been there for 1 week

it has become a slouch, a pucker, a color lowercase doesn't know, a demented tangerine, an explosion of magenta-rot, odorless and cold, a burst of citrus-vein, a flabby dimpled ass, a cup of stringy soup

the orange sits on her dashboard
it has been there for 2 weeks

it is trying to say something meaningful, losing pocks by the millisecond, giving her bad advice about bed skirts, drowning in regret, leaving her again and again, ignoring her puffy eyes, moving to a different state, slobbering down the dash, no longer sweet or round or there for her

the orange has packed its things in a mini-valise, hitchhiked to ocala, and refuses to forward its new address

just another day in '82

l.c.'s father is out in the yard yanking weeds from his shit-baked lawn.
he plucks only three among millions before stopping for a smoke.
he pulls a pack of winstons from the chest pocket of his worn flannel,
lights one, and hacks up a ball of phlegm as he exhales.

l.c.'s mum is inside viciously crocheting a baby bonnet for whomever-
gets-knocked-up-next while her pot full of brussels sprouts bubbles over
on the stove. in minutes, her father will drag his gin-red-face inside
and force her to pray over food she despises.

l.c. is in her bedroom staring at a half-naked poster of matt dillon.
her diary is open and she draws 5 red lines underneath the word diet.
when the garbagy smell of brussels sprouts causes her to retch and gag,
she jabs a rusted diaper pin into her cottage cheesy thigh and bleeds.

qu-qu-quench
"what size do you want to be?" the caterpillar asked.

lowercase unlocks
her abalone knife
and slices hunks
of dead skin
from the balls
of her feet

*

exfoliates
breaks the crusted
loofah in half
and pares down her face
almond freckles
plink like sunflower seeds
into the ringed basin

*

succumbs (lowercase always succumbs)
arches over the bowl
like a saggy mushroom
and waits for the tingle
of synapses to tremble
through the rose of her cheeks

*

deflate
lowercase likes what she sees
the alice-shrivel
the infinitesimal
brilliance of small

*
beaming
lowercase stands in the center
of the aluminum
trash barrel
and indulges in echo
you are dwindle
you are so, so, good

fumes

what was that musty smell rainwater dead mice why did they keep the rusted old car in the garage and the newer one outside she wants know what she was wearing her flannel pjs her sweatpants a goddamn tutu who stirred! i said who stirred! did the wooden steps creak as she made her way down were the car keys jangling in her pocket as she crept honestly can you look her straight in the eye and tell her that no one heard those jangling keys what made her slip the missing tread and had she even taken time to write a note a list of who gets what lazy so lazy lazy with a capital l why was the vinyl seat so cold when she first climbed in was it winter was it 3:00am could she see her breath and was that freaking tv still yammering up there did she sit for a while on the cold seat before turning the engine on you mean to tell me no one upstairs heard the rumble of that engine who was home anyway she wants to know who was home and why did the thought of her cat stalking finches make her bawl was it a school night was her homework done (that's a joke!) why can she still see that purple gods-eye dangling from the rearview mirror did she switch off the engine after ten minutes or five is she making all this up can you hear her is she deaf is she speaking in tongues are her lips moving is she stuttering are you saying that she's nuts and those thick nauseating fumes was she dizzy did she puke what made her stop are you serious not one person upstairs heard the thunder of the car engine through those drafty floors and were the brown creepy spiders watching her—she coughed right?

(hey, sunflower, l.c. thinks you might be dead)

the water in your rattlesnake vase is hushed.
she cannot hear your vermin taps across the kitchen floor.
the word floret does not tempt her.
she's lifting the blinds and peeking at you dear sepia fleur-
among the rubble on the winter-soaked porch.
she keeps mistaking you for a honeycomb,
she keeps mistaking you for an abandoned wasp palace,
death inside of her mouth, your voice a breath choking on wood pulp.
she's been sleeping more and consulting the mirror less.
because the sickly stick trees said you are.

the day lowercase heard her brother tell ricky c he wanted her dead

she hid in the coke bottle vase stuffed with droopy backyard forsythias he purposely knocked off the table when he discovered she had eaten the last friggin' oreo   she hid in the mangled toilet paper tube in his filthy hamster cage where all those hairless squirming babies died of starvation   she hid in the eye socket of the drool crusted teddy bear he whacked her with when she scratched his scary monsters record   she hid in the joke of a padlock on his bedroom door she picked clean with one of bernadette's greasy bobby pins   she hid in the armpit of his precious black cure t-shirt she stole from the hamper, stretched, and wore in the over chlorinated pool (you have to admit robert smith's succulent red lips morphing into flaming swiss cheese was sublime)   she hid in the spine of the crinkled dirty magazine she found in the fort he built with the shittiest plywood ever   she hid in the delicious layer of chocolate on the charleston chew candy bar he never gave her half of because he said she needed to lose a few   she hid in the flip-top lid of the rolling stones butane lighter he singed her baby crissy's long retractable hair with   she hid in the thumbprint of fluff he left on the volume knob on her bumble bee yellow 8-track player   she hid in the knuckles of his bony tanorama fist that punched her in her fleshy places   she hid in the bruises that spread like moldering sunflowers beneath her long sleeved and way-too-hot-for-summer tops   she hid in the can of hot sticky fresca and nail clippings he forced her to swig from in front of the freaky deaky bronstein brothers.

from haiku to thwack

click   echo   click, click

    home?   unbridledheelclick

        ruby dread slippers

            can't stop him

                from slapping her appleless

numbering the gruesome

one. shut it. we are about to get jiggy in plumblood.

two. what does blood do when it's forced from a face?

three. does blood have wet dreams?

four. he drove around in that blue-as-his-eyes, blue-as-his-fist trans am. he drove around in a wet dream fizz prowling for plumblood.

five. and all for a bag of piss warm beer.

six. and all for a bag of piss warm beer.

seven. l.c. was 16 and kept herself.

eight. l.c. was 16, kept to herself, and drew sunflowers on her jeans with a ballpoint pen.

nine. he was 16 too.

ten. he was 16, drove a blue trans am, and worked his pretty blue eyes on pretty blond girls.

eleven. l.c. was not blond, and she wasn't very pretty.

twelve. dank parking lot. revved up trans am. piss warm beer. thirsty teenage boy.

thirteen. *give me the bag, fats.* l.c. said, *no.* he asked again. she said, *no.*

fourteen. gush. with a blow to the face—blood will gush.

fifteen. did i mention her nose?

sixteen. it slipped like a yolk down the slope of her cheek.

like a canker it came running

that was the spring she decided. a plan unraveled from inside her. she tricked all the mirrors. nicked them with kitchen knives. made parts of her pay. she came close to lopping. grabbed fistfuls of droopy hip and squeezed. there was so much shoved in that begged to come out. it wasn't supposed to last. but what starts out as seed, (even sickly, spongesoppy seed) blooms. it got so bad that the knives rebelled and dulled, and she was forced to use her teeth, even the yuckmucky rotten ones. teeth against glass? when her teeth were all gone, paired down to grim nubs, she plucked out the bones in her sore and sorry mouth. one by one she washed off the ticks of meat and dark moussey cake. dried them by the mushrooming fire. she spent more than a fortnight sharpening her bones into stickpins shaped like her anger. it was fun. it was yummy fun. then one afternoon, when the dastardly world was at work, she jabbed each and every one those bones into her fatty, fatty heart.

b-b-bladespeak

petal

it started   dark   unable
a kitchenette   scarred   verdurous
formica   elbowed cold   kill
those nights   she'd kill for   capiz vase
fresh cut   drop leaf   cat scratched deep
wood   she'd kill for   damp sunflower
chalked rings   butterridges   sick amounts
of giddy up   happy   pills   she seeds this   not
that   the sunflowers   real   and petals
floating stiffly   face up

a night by the sink

it's after 2a.m. and in waltzes goldenboy, hair across his golden ass, tight faded levis, straw cowboy hat worn and split in just the right places. lowercase is standing by the kitchen sink. the window above the sink is open, and she is smitten with cricket-song. but wait—lowercase doesn't give a shit about nature, maybe she's high. goldenboy reeks of something stronger than beer, and his eyes are blazing. goldenboy staggers to the refrigerator, slips on mum's wicked shiny floor, catches himself, but doesn't fall. lowercase makes a noise that isn't quite a chuckle. goldenboy disappears from the kitchen, and returns with his hunting rifle. he rests the muzzle of the rifle against lowercase's moist temple, cocks it, and she tries not to breathe. slowly, goldenboy counts out loud to ten, burps real loud, and withdraws. goldenboy makes a noise that it isn't quite a chuckle.

exhuming the thrum

splash of nepenthe, mummy unquickens.
beneath her frown-dewy-neck,
l.c.'s triangular tip scalpels in.

the x-acto slopes and three swift nicks.
she eases off a stitch of mummy's breast-skin,
and places it on a dish in the sink.

the mashy threads crackle,
as she rakes through mummy's cage,
and calls out for her heart.

numb to her, always numb to her
l.c.'s gelid tool careens
along the slip of her ribs.

this gets messy, sticky, hostile.
she has impaled her pale,
and cannot stop.

l.c. unearths a bump tangled in stemgut.
it is too small to sweat a real pulse,
so she leaves it intact. grateful for the thrum.

as l.c. is folding in her drying flaps
and thumbnursing her cuts,
mummy comes to.

thanksgiving murk

and the lord said splash some sun you dolt you pledget you b-side scratch on the sofa the lord said you will become one with thread and the parts of your body that protrude will make the slipcover flaccid like pudding so the lord said i will give you two lives the first to wash and wring the second permanent press and in the second you shall use adverbs like tumidly freely and you will stand with your ear to the great cherry door and listen as the children grouse and you will not blink or knuckle under like a sissy as the takers pluck hair from the lattice of your lungs and the woman with the crooked toes exactly like yours stuffs all the ziploc baggies with meat and stuffing and cookies shaped like turkeys and you will not be tempted you will not flinch or whine you will not be roused the lord the lord the lord with his clipped tongue and meaningful ways wills you to scrape mashed potatoes and hardened squash wills you to steel-wool the splutter of gravy around the left rear burner the lord wills you to wrap up the remaining biscuits smash those godamned gold rimmed dinner plates and move on.

8th floor

do the clumps of snow shivering on the cement ledge--does the crushed paper cup or the balled up mottled tissue--do the lulls of consecrated quiet--does the bleach spotted johnny--does the translucent shoulder--does the reality of what's been done--do the strands of glossy auburn hair slipping from the nurse's coral barrette--do the limp burning hands--does the barbaric tape hastily clutching the tube against an ivory throat--does the awkward swell of meaningless chatter--does the hovering winter sun washing over everything in the sterile room--do the dog-eared pages of ariel--does the skittish cat that never leaves the closet--do the lightly crusted gashes on fleshy upper arms--do the teensy quakes of envy buried in tangled psyches--does the knotted silk scarf resting on a collarbone or the thick stink of vodka and cigarettes--does the red bloated kielbasa tongue sleeping on a porcelain cheek--does the word attempt mean there was no intention--does the gauzy cotton blanket wrapped tightly around a flaccid body--do the scant flutterings beneath opaline lids--does the loosened stitch on a salt stained leather boot--do the empty pill bottles lolling around on the dresser--do the swooping gulls or the breathlessly azure sky--does the stuck zipper on a pea green coat--does the answering machine with the eerie message--do the shiny cars parked in little slanted rows?

lowercase in sunflower headdress

lowercase buckles something copper under her chin, and sits in front of the mirror, surprised by the bewitching sight of herself.

at first her reflection reads featherlicious, all gosling fluffied, lemon zesty, and velvety gamboge sun.

lowercase scooches up close to the mirror and without any provocation whatsoever, each pore on her face opens wide. she punches a grubby fist inside each dank hovel her face has to offer—

and looks beyond seed and corolla. super 8 film footage flashes and blinks. lowercase sees herself in second grade hiding behind a shivering oak tree in a too-tight nautical one-piece bathing suit that makes her look like a ship.

more flashes. lowercase catches sight of herself in every other grade—creeping about, watching her orca step, always on the lookout for places to crawl into—places without light.

lowercase unbuckles lickety-split. the headdress thunks when it hits the floor. back to the truth with a heave and a hoe. big, graceless, hide-in-the-bush-bloom, unable to attract anything but weed whackers and rodents.

off the mark

call her bad diet.
call her manitoba and giggly onset.
never call her some bloody minion.
call her popcorn meatball,
and 3a.m. bowl of dinty moore.
you have entered the galley of rooster timers-
and beaded pelican mitts,
and she is swatting at her brother's sickening shadows.
his cologne is eighth grade.
his cologne is guy unsmiley.
his cologne is mr. gorham picking his nose
behind the portable chalkboard, and rubbing it
on his wide wale cords.
i think i love you. so, what am i so afraid of?
i'm afraid that i'm not sure of; a love there is no cure for.
and he heard her sing it into her david cassidy pillow.
and he saw her drool and kiss
his shiny feathered hair—way too hard.
when she sees him now she bolts.
when she sees him now she goosesteps
through his widening eye bags.
it's way too late to tell on him for flicking
the 3-legged guinea pig in the throat.
he was so in love with his 80's midriff boy-tees
that bought him girls with bakelite bangles
yowling at his bedroom door.
hey there, strawberry boones farm.
hey there, golden gloat of pig ear dangle.
you said her gross feet would land her
in a prison of cat piss.
you said you'd smother her
in a nest of macramé door owls
if she ever breathed a fucking word.

b-b-bladespeak

gelid. an icicle stabbing a dove. exacting.
taut as it sniffs out the spot. clean as a dribble
of blood on a pin. never say no and never ask why,
and it releases you. tip of it searing you—and then
rush again, split again, swell again, feel again.
glisten and tingle and icicles clamoring.
something is wrong with it. numb to the cut and it's
numb to the sore, and its gluttonous pine for you.
skin, it should dull and then rust for you, stop you from
slicing it. curtail this incising, delighting.
nape on your thumb and it's edge in your sweat.
it is hope, it is light, it is rouse, it is icicle weeping
for vanishing, trembling, guileless, guileless love?

getting to white

and this is a poem for l.c.   the question is   why would she blind into white   these are the tiles   this is not about color   the hushing the purling   that is not the question   she stood in the water and pruned into white   a gauntly tale   what is the sound of a glutinous sud   the smell of a pearl   the scene behind spumy lids   these are the tiles   she lathered and soaped   lathered and sopped   it she sane   hush!   the cocking was drenched   the sweet-sizzle-steam her motive   that is not the question   blanched hands reaching   the furling light   the question is   will she ever be happy   the shampoo, (a coconut white)   these are the tiles don't forget about the bleach   the steam unfolding   the wettest gardenias   that is not the question   she imagines the white   she is gathering the white   she slipped on the white   the mizzly pills dissolving like dew down her throat   she's a drench   shush!   the question is   is she foaming at the bones   gripping the towel rack shushing herself to the size of a scrub   is she sane   and what about her tooth   can the purling white   the lathery white   the bleach-bone-spumy-white   bleed with the red   does a slip on the suds make the sound of a bone   the question is   is there really a question   these are the tiles   the blood   the tooth   the soap and the slip   these are the tiles   this is not about color   and this is a poem for l.c.

truths and half-truths about sunflowers

one. there are two kinds of sunflowers: the sunflowers you find in books and poems and the sunflowers that chew through phone wire.

two. when a sunflower looks at itself in the mirror, it does not see gold or ochre or tourmaline.

three. most believe that sunflowers move towards the light. lowercase believes that light moves towards the sunflowers.

four. with stems as thick as femurs.

five. the scratching you hear at night is not the cat or wind or the flaccid branches of the silk tree.

six. never leave sunflowers alone with purple love-grass, pink parfait roses, or baby's-breath.

seven. what is the difference between a slouch and a lurch?

eight. slaked with fuzz and blue-green rot, a sunflower will still have the strength to hobble to the foot of your bed.

nine. on the twenty-seventh day of this insufferable heat lowercase will no longer know where the sunflower ends and everything else begins.

ABOUT THE AUTHOR

Christine Tierney's poems and flash fiction have appeared in *Fourteen Hills, Poet Lore, PMS, The Tusculum Review, Permafrost, LEVELER, Sugar House Review* and elsewhere. She holds an MFA from The University of Southern Maine's Stonecoast Writing Program, and a BA in film from Emerson College. Her work has been nominated for Best of the Net, a Pushcart Prize, and the Best New Poets Anthology. She is employed as an afterschool director. She is a funk and disco lover, and also a wannabe comedian.

www.ingramcontent.com/pod-product-compliance
Lightning Source LLC
Chambersburg PA
CBHW021131080526
44587CB00012B/1232